Published in Australia in 2020 by SisterShip Training Pty Ltd

www.sistershiptraining.com

Copyright © SisterShip Training Pty Ltd 2020

All rights reserved. Without limiting the rights under copyright above, no part of this publication may be reproduced, stored in or introduced into a retrieval system, or transmitted in any form or by any means (electronic, mechanical, photocopying, recording, or otherwise), without prior written permission of both the copyright owner/the Publisher.

National Library of Australia data:

SisterShip Training Pty Ltd, 2020, Passage Planning with E-Charts

ISBN: 978-0-6451815-2-4

www.sistershiptraining.com

Contents

INTRODUCTION 1
   Navigation 1
   Ocean miles & passages 1
   What is passage planning? 1

THE FOUNDATIONS OF A PASSAGE PLAN 3
   Considerations 3
   Contingency Plans 3
   Resources: 3
   Planning a Safe Course 4

ELEMENTS OF PASSAGE PLAN 4
   Appraisal 4
   Planning 5
   Execution 6
   Monitoring 6

Section Summary 7

APPENDIX 8
   Chart Planning Example 8
   Position Fixing - Bearings 10
   Chart work 11
   Harbour Considerations 14
   Electronic Navigation Aids 14
   Log Book 14
   Crew 15
   Rules of the Watch/Standing Orders 17
   Summary of Responsible Navigational Practices 18
   Parallel Indexing Using Radar 18
   Bearings 19
   Emergency Preparation 21

CHECKLISTS 21
   Pre-Departure Checklists (Extended Cruise) 21
   Navigation 22
   Day before departure 22
   Navigation Check List 23
   Routine Checks 24
   Daily Checks When Underway 25

Examples of Appraisal Information 27
   PLANNING 27

- Radar: 27
- Charts 27
- Speeds 27
- Depth Sounder 27

THE THEORY OF TIDES 28
- What Causes Tides? 28
- Chart Datum 29
- Tide Duration and Range 30
- Standard Ports 30
- Tide Tables 30
- Standard Port 30
- Heights and Times of Intermediate Tides 31
  - Intermediate Heights Example: 31
- Determining Under Keel Clearance 33
- The formula 34
- Under Keel Clearance Example 34

Section Summary 35

INTRODUCTION TO ELECTRONIC CHARTS 36

An Introduction to ENCs Capabilities and Limitations 37
- Survey 37
- The Zoom Function 37
- GPS 39

Disasters 40

The Different Charts 42

Satellite Programs 42

Important 42

Appendix 43
- The Pros/The Cons of Electronic Charts 43

The Official Line from AMSA / IMO / HYDROGRAPHIC OFFICE 45
- Scale 45

Official Australian nautical charts 45
- Unofficial nautical charts 45
- Unofficial ENCs 46
- Australian nautical charts and publications 47
- From AMSA: SOLAS Chapter V 47

Further Reading 48

Acknowledgements 48

Disclaimer 48

INTRODUCTION

Navigation

Planning your trip is fun, but it is also a serious task and incredibly helpful, especially when those unexpected challenges create a twist in the journey. Your mind should fully explore where you plan to take your boat and crew.

All the information together with preparing for your journey can be overwhelming, but it is far better to have a good handle on the data pertinent to your trip at the start, before you untie the lines.

You cannot sufficiently passage plan on electronic charts alone. You must view and study the big picture on paper charts. It is beneficial to plan using both paper charts and electronic charts.

Ocean miles & passages

Your confidence will grow over time. Knowing you have a seaworthy boat, systems, rigging, sails, and an idea of what you are doing (because you have researched, read, and completed courses).

The best way to build your confidence is by doing lots of sea miles. The sooner you leave, the sooner you will gain your confidence. Even after many years of sailing many miles and being around a vast array of boats, Noel and I always feel a little anxious before departing for a voyage and on longer journeys it can take a couple of days to settle into the travelling rhythm. There's nothing wrong with this, it keeps us alert. Ocean miles can be easier than coastal miles; there are fewer things to hit!

What is passage planning?

When we fly or drive somewhere we check times, luggage, insurance, the route etc. It's no different for a voyage at sea whether coastal or offshore.

Passage Plans are a crucial part of going to sea. Time spent on preparation is key to a safe, rewarding, and satisfying voyage. It could also mean the difference between disaster and a successful voyage.

A Passage Plan is a written plan for going to sea. It is a comprehensive, berth to berth guide, developed and used by a vessel's skipper and crew to determine:

- The most favourable route with safety and speed; the vessel's ability; and the crew's ability taken into account.
- Potential problems or hazards along the route.
- Allocated tasks in an emergency.
- Abiding to local and international rules and regulations.

Speed directly affects your arrival time. Arriving into port at night or close to dusk is a big consideration. Do you understand the buoyage system? Is it a safe entry for night time? Familiarise yourself with the port's entrance lights and sequence before you arrive.

Throughout this course, we will look at a number of different pilotage techniques, cross-checking, and utilising many skills to provide you with the safest navigation.

Transits, bearings, tidal height, clearance bearings are all important and extremely useful skills to learn and use. The Passage Plan, in this course, will be as detailed as a commercial vessel's plan, often your plan (recreational) will be shorter without the commercial legalities and detail. We'll cover all bases on this course and it is up to you to decide on the depth of planning you undertake. You are, of course, responsible for your learning, set up, and planning. This is only showing you how we planned for our voyages.

SisterShip Training and its employees and tutors cannot be held responsible for your time and safety on the water. This is only advice, how you use it and how much of it you use is entirely up to you, it's your responsibility.

THE FOUNDATIONS OF A PASSAGE PLAN

It's Common Sense
Collect information. Some will be approximate, but most will need to be accurate. Of course, readiness for any eventuality is the key.

Considerations
- Weather forecast
- Tides (effect on vessel)
- Wind (effect on vessel)
- Fuel consumption / measuring remaining fuel / planning
- Boat limitations
- Crew limitations (crew experience and physical condition)
- Safety equipment on board
- Navigational dangers including shipping lanes and narrow passages
- Boat maintenance equipment / spares
- Paperwork
- Provisions/victualing
- A trustworthy person onshore with all your details
- Utilising different navigation tools and skills

Contingency Plans
Contingency plans are imperative in case of an emergency, noting the potential bolt-holes along the way will help ease what could be a stressful situation. What if someone becomes ill? Or is injured? You may suffer mechanical problems or the weather deteriorates, forcing you to change your plans or seek out a safe harbour.

When it comes to your navigational plan, plot waypoints and ensure they are appropriate for the time of day you will be travelling and the forecast conditions.

Always inform someone ashore of your plans, in detail. Advise them of the procedures should they be concerned for your welfare, and give them a copy of your passage plan.

Recommended reading: Viki Moore (https://astrolabesailing.com/)

Resources:
- Over all planning chart
- Charts for entire trip
- Detailed port chart of destination and possible contingencies
- Detailed approach channel chart
- Almanac (or App) for tidal heights, tidal streams, and port data
- Pilot books for photos and local knowledge
- Weather Forecast and location of good shelter
- Radio frequencies for destination port and back up ports

Passage Details (write them out):
- Departure time/location
- Proposed destination and arrival date/time
- Type of vessel (for most of us this will not change and we should know her capabilities in various conditions and handling characteristics)
- Details of vessel
  - Fuel capacity (litres per hour consumed in varying conditions) and status
  - Water capacity and status
  - Sails
  - Equipment
  - Cruising speed, under sailing/motor
  - Draft

Weather forecast

Check the local forecast and the bigger picture, i.e. synoptic charts. The Bureau of Meteorology (BOM) supplies long range weather forecasts, as does WeatherFax. Synoptic charts provide the overall picture so you can monitor and follow any developing systems. Check local weather too.

Planning a Safe Course

Successful navigation is represented by: **KNOWLEDGE: JUDGEMENT: AWARENESS**

ELEMENTS OF PASSAGE PLAN

The essential steps are:
- Appraisal
- Planning
- Execution
- Monitoring

Appraisal

To begin, the destination is agreed upon with a discussion on distance and timing (both length of voyage and seasonal timing). General research is required at this stage, on the port, length of stay, visas required (if another country), cost, etc., to ensure the trip is feasible/possible.

- Gather all information on the proposed passage
- Ascertain risks
- Purchase and study publications
- Online research (e.g. https://www.noonsite.com/)

This involves information extracted from publications as well as those within the chart. The appraisal can include some/all details from (dependent on area/reason for voyage e.g. delivery, commercial work):
- Chart Catalogues
- Charts
- Ocean Passages of The World
- Routeing Charts
- Port information booklets/State handbooks
- Admiralty Sailing Directions
- Admiralty List of Lights and Fog Signals
- Admiralty List of Radio Signals

- Tide Tables
- Tidal Stream Atlas
- Notices to Mariners
- Admiralty Distance Tables
- Ships Routeing
- Navigational Warnings
- Mariner's Handbook
- Draft of Ship
- Owners and other sources
- Personal Experience
- Electronic equipment manuals
- Owner's handbook/Safety Management Systems

Usually for longer distances the course is first laid off on a small-scale chart to view the entire picture. Later this can be transferred to larger scale charts (i.e. more detail) where amendments can be made.

Planning

Once you have made a full appraisal with all the information at hand you are now ready to plan the passage. The route is marked out from berth to berth (or port to port if on anchor).

Highlight/note dangerous areas such as:
- Reefs
- Small islands
- Wrecks
- Shallow waters
- And any information that may aid safe navigation such as safe turning points, back up anchor sites or ports, e.g. find and note emergency anchor positions.

Work out when you are sailing at night and during the day. Note light sequences for night time coastal sailing and obvious landmarks for daytime.

If you have radar, note suitable places to take ranges from, note these on your course line/chart so you can swiftly double check your position along the way. Use parallel indexing (if you have radar onboard).

Other areas to make notes of:
- No-go areas
- Margins of safety
- Charted tracks
- Course alterations/distance
- Bearings/course
- Parallel indexing
- Aborts and contingencies
- Clearing line and bearings
- Leading lines
- Tides and current
- Change in engine status
- Minimum under keel clearance (UKC)
- Use of depth sounder
- Natural Transits

Abort Points: When approaching narrow or constrained waterways, the vessel might be in a position in which there is no possible action but to proceed. For example, the vessel enters an area so narrow there is no room to turn around. For this purpose, a position is drawn on the chart showing the last point within the passage that you can abort (i.e. turn around).

Contingencies: Events don't always go as planned, so we account for these situations where possible. Contingencies include:

> - Safe anchorages
> - Waiting areas
> - Alternative routes
> - Emergency marinas/berths
> - Alternative port

Cautionary Notes: e.g. is there a Military fire practice area that requires additional lookout and a more active radio monitoring?

Organisation: Group the relevant charts together in order of use.

Up to date: Ensure charts and publications have been updated where necessary, e.g. Notice to Marinas.

Waypoints: Waypoints are useful as reference points or a track. Plan your route on a small scale paper chart to view the complete picture. Once the latitude/longitude of the waypoints are entered into the GPS transfer waypoints to large scale charts (or to your e-charts). It's good practice to check your waypoints with a range and bearing if possible.

Note: When changing paper charts carefully study the scale and plot the last plot on the previous chart onto the new chart – carefully double checking for accuracy.

Execution
Following the plan. Prepare the vessel: Stow your gear, Provision, Press up tanks (ensure they are full), Clear decks, Ready to sail.

ETAs: Consider the time of arrival with favourable tidal streams, daylight. Perhaps you are entering a coral reef and it is necessary to have the sun behind you to navigate your way through.

Standing Orders: Each skipper will have their own standards and expectations. (Intro details – and call when approach coast, passing narrow waterways – engine status change (speed up/slow down), sail change? Bad weather, heavy traffic.)

Monitoring
The plan is in place and you are underway. Now it is a simple task to monitor your progress utilising your plan, e.g.:

> - Checking your position (GPS/three-bearing fix/distance and bearing)
> - Ensure you remain a safe distance away from hazards
> - Utilise parallel indexing, to maintain safe distances

- Your plan will help keep the vessel save. If situations arise where you have to deviate from the plan, it is a good idea to discuss, with your crew, the pros and cons, using all available knowledge, judgement, and seamanship.
- Conform to Collision Regulations
- Maintain situational awareness, a proper lookout includes by sight and sound.

Section Summary

This introduction to Passage Planning is a good start to help you prepare a comprehensive coastal passage considering safe navigation. You've covered some safety points, e.g. narrow waterways and shallow depths. You've also learned to plan for un-planned stoppages/anchoring and consider equipment failure.

APPENDIX

Chart Planning Example

See Image 1: Extract of Planning Chart (Australian Index of Nautical Charts) AUS5000

You are required to sail your vessel to Dunk Island from Cairns. What charts and publications would you order?

Lay off your course and select the charts required, e.g.
AUS262, AUS830, AUS829, AUS258 (back up), AUS828, AUS258, AUS 259 (back up)

The main publications are a pilot book, either via a private author (Lucas) or a government publication, e.g. Australian Pilot Vol 111, the Australian National Tide Tables, and Admiralty Charts and Symbols book NP5011.

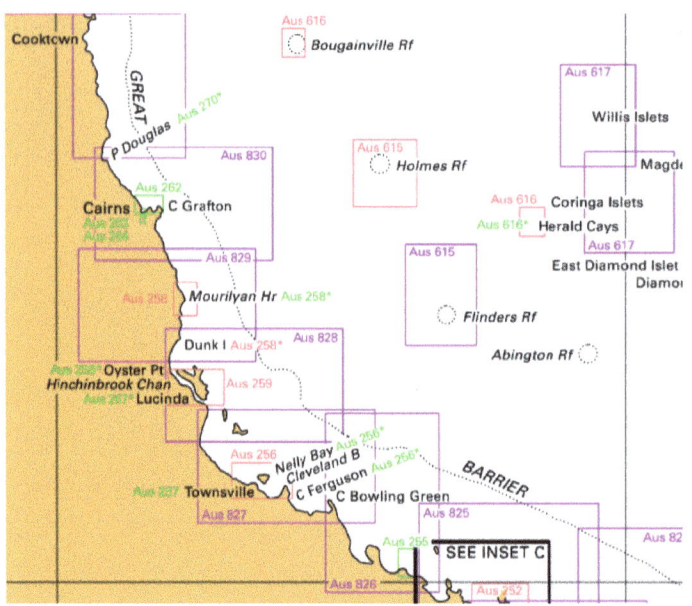

Image 1: Extract from Planning Chart (Australian Index of Nautical Charts) AUS5000

When purchasing charts ensure they are corrected to the latest Notices to Mariners. Study the charts with reference to your publications.

Use the largest scales available commensurate with your route. Check the sounding measurements are in metres (older charts or USA charts could be feet or fathoms).

Read the various notes and warnings on your chart and mark those applicable to your route, e.g. Zone of Confidence rating.

Lay off suitable courses from your departure position to your finish position.

You will find that more than one course will be required to your destination, and therefore the selection of the route must combine economy with safety. The shortest distance can be used only if it is safe.

If coastal cruising, lay off your course considering the following:

- Pass close enough to the shore to make certain of seeing and identifying all prominent landmarks, such as lighthouses and beacons, and obtain frequent fixes.

- Keep well clear of hazards and dangers.

- If you decide that 5 metres is your minimum sounding, on the chart mark around dangers.

Mark around dangers along your route

- Note which part of your journey will be in daylight and which in darkness. With limited navigational aids, it may be prudent to go further away from the coastline at night, but remain within the range of lights.

- Make allowances for the forecast meteorological conditions.

- Study the wind, tide and currents, what effect will they have on your vessel?

- Never pass a light without checking its period and characteristic.

- Do not fix your position by buoys or other floating aids when other objects are available. Buoys marking shoals may be moved as the shoal extends and this information may take some time to be broadcast. Or a buoy may have been accidentally moved.

- Remember currents and tidal streams often follow coastlines.

- Caution must be applied near and around acceleration zones (an acceleration zone is high ground which rises abruptly, or between two islands where the wind funnels through).

- If you transfer from one chart to another, check the scales careful, they may differ. Transfer your position by bearing and distance of a well charted point common to both charts. Then check that plot via latitude and longitude and ensure they are the same on both charts.

- If possible, where you change course along your route, select the alteration to occur when two features are in transit or a conspicuous feature is abeam.

- Fix your position via objects that are close to you.

- When in narrow waterways allow plenty of room when rounding points of land, buoys, shoals. NEVER cut corners, it is dangerous.

- While rounding buoys observe the buoys to double check the direction and speed of the tide.

- When rounding buoys to windward and against the stream, always give them a wide berth. If there is clear water on all sides, pass downstream of them, you may underestimate the strength of tidal stream.

- When passing between islands and fixing your position use objects which are all on the same land. The two islands may have been separately surveyed.

Position Fixing - Bearings
When taking bearings of low points of land, errors may occur unless the High Water Mark (Chartered Coastline) is clearly defined.

This error is emphasised when there is a large tidal range and the beach gradient is small.

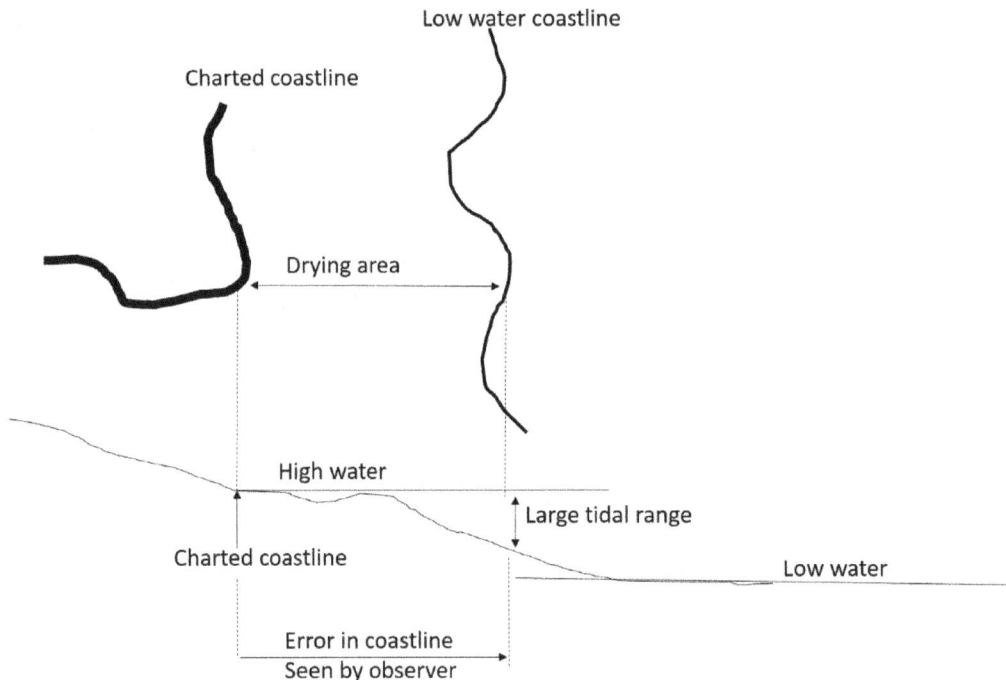

Consider traffic density. Give larger vessels plenty of room especially in areas of shallow and narrow areas. Carry a copy of the Collision Regulations on board so you can easily identify any signals the larger vessel is carrying, e.g. constrained by draft and restricted in ability to manoeuvre.

Traversing narrow passages or in-close to reef areas, positions can be taken every two or three minutes if necessary but not so as to cause confusion. This is best done with a large-scale chart and more than one person (if possible).

Radar has priority over GPS in narrow waters. Using distance-off points to ensure the radar is on the lowest range possible so that all aspects of the track can be viewed. Change ranges (up and down) to ensure you know what is happening around you.

Do not put the vessel into a dangerous situation at any time. If you are not 100% sure of the situation stay clear of all dangers and if you are uncertain of where you are STOP until you have found out where you are and are sure of your next action.

If your chart has a Zone of Confidence diagram, study the picture and table information in relation to your route. AUS252 (ZOC) below:

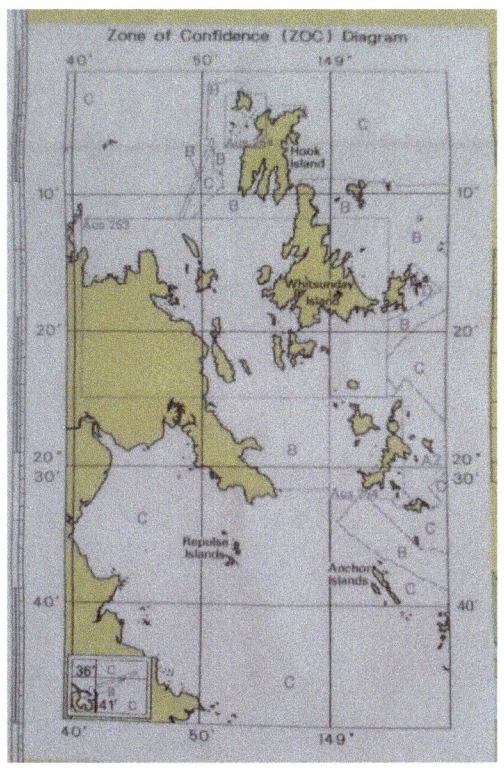

ZOC	POSITION ACCURACY	DEPTH ACCURACY	SEAFLOOR COVERAGE
A1	±5m	=0·50m + 1%d	Significant seafloor features detected
A2	±20m	=1·00m + 2%d	Significant seafloor features detected
B	±50m	=1·00m + 2%d	Uncharted features hazardous to surface navigation are not expected but may exist
C	±500m	=2·00m + 5%d	Depth anomalies may be expected
D	Worse than ZOC C	Worse than ZOC C	Large depth anomalies may be expected
U	Unassessed - The quality of the bathymetric data has yet to be assessed.		

ZOC CATEGORIES
(For details see Seafarers Handbook for Australian Waters AHP 20)

Chart work

Charts come in different scales:

Planning charts are typically 1:10,000,000, covering large areas such as the Indian Ocean, North Pacific etc. The shoreline and topography is not shown in great detail. Used for planning and position fixing on long ocean passages.

Ocean Charts are typically 1:10,000,000, these are for planning and position fixing on off-shore ocean passages, e.g. Pacific Ocean.

General Charts are typically 1:1,000,000 and used for coastal navigation.

Coastal Charts are typically 1:150,000 and used for inshore navigation.

Plan Charts are typically 1:75,000 with insets of 1:37,500 and provide greater detail of harbours and rivers.

For harbours and rivers giving great detail, example: AUS 32 Cambridge Gulf 1:75,000 with insets of 1:37,500 Wyndham Approaches and 1:7,500 Wyndham Wharf.

- Ensure all charts are corrected to the latest Notices to Mariners.
- Study your charts together with your publications.
- Use the largest scale charts available commensurate with the route.
- Are the sounding feet, metres, fathoms – highlight.
- Read all the notes and highlight those pertinent to your route.
- Lay off your course from departure point to destination – combine safety with economy.
- Highlight hazards on chart, reefs, shallow water.
- Mark out danger areas and note bearings if you can (of any dangers).
- Box off danger areas with clearing bearings.
- Plot waypoints and ensure they are appropriate for the time of day you will be travelling and the forecast conditions. This is best done prior to entering them in to the GPS.
- Enter way points into GPS – double check them.
- Never entirely rely on GPS. Commercial vessels and recreational vessels in NSW, South Australia, and Northern Territory, by law, must have official charts on board (historically paper charts were a requirement, but electronic charts are acceptable providing they are the Official Charts (e.g. from the Hydrographic Office) and the vessel has a second Electronic Chart Display System (ECDIS), connected to an independent power supply and a separate Global Navigation Satellite Systems (GNSS) position input (the back up system can still be paper charts, providing they are official charts. All types of charts must be kept up to date.

Quote from the Hydrographic Office (Australia): "Recreational Vessels: In New South Wales, Northern Territory and South Australia it is a requirement to carry an official chart when going offshore or beyond smooth waters. In all other States it is recommended as good practice. AusENC and ARCS, when kept up-to-date, will allow recreational vessels to meet state electronic chart regulations. See the table below for further details:

AusENC are the official Electronic Navigation Charts (from the Hydrographic Office
ARCS are the official Admiralty Raster Chart Service from the UK Hydrographic Office

STATE	CARRIAGE REQUIREMENTS (CHARTS)	MARINE AUTHORITIES
New South Wales	Required for open waters	NSW Roads and Maritime Services www.maritime.nsw.gov.au
Queensland	Recommended for smooth, partially smooth, and beyond smooth waters.	Maritime Safety Queensland www.msq.qld.gov.au
Victoria	Advisable for all waters	Transport Safety Victoria www.transportsafety.vic.gov.au
South Australia	Unprotected waters All vessels > 10 nautical miles from shore	Department of Planning, Transport and Infrastructure www.transport.sa.gov.au
Northern Territory	Vessels > 5 metres	Northern Territory Government information and services – boating Fishing and Marine https://nt.gov.au/marine/marine-safety
Tasmania	Advisable for all waters	Department of Planning, Transport and Infrastructure www.transport.sa.gov.au

AusENC are protected under the Hydrographic Office data protection scheme (S-63). An IHO S-63 compatible system is required to use AusENC. (IHO is the International Hydrographic Organization)

ARCS are encrypted with Hydrographic Chart Raster Format (HCRF) format. A navigation system must be ARCS compatible to use these charts.

- While most states recommend paper charts you can be sure that if an incident occurs your insurance company and investigators will be checking for appropriate navigation tools. GPS isn't infallible with both the signal and the accuracy potentially vulnerable. They can just stop working at the most inconvenient times too and your batteries could fail. Unofficial chart providers carry a disclaimer stating their charts are not for navigation purposes.

- You must know how to navigate to safety should the GPS fail. Knowing exactly where you are at all times is crucial (and if you are in any doubt whatsoever remember to stop and establish your position).

- Familiarise yourself with landmarks along your route.

- Calculate the compass course to steer using the Variation from the chart and the Deviation for your boat, prior to leaving.

- Have a portable (plastic coated) chart in the cockpit if you can.

- Put what you see on your chart into reality. The diagram below shows nautical miles broken down into tenths. While they look small, one tenth of a nautical mile is 185 metres, so half of one tenth is a little over 90 metres. Out at sea this is can be irrelevant but in a narrow channel this could be critical.

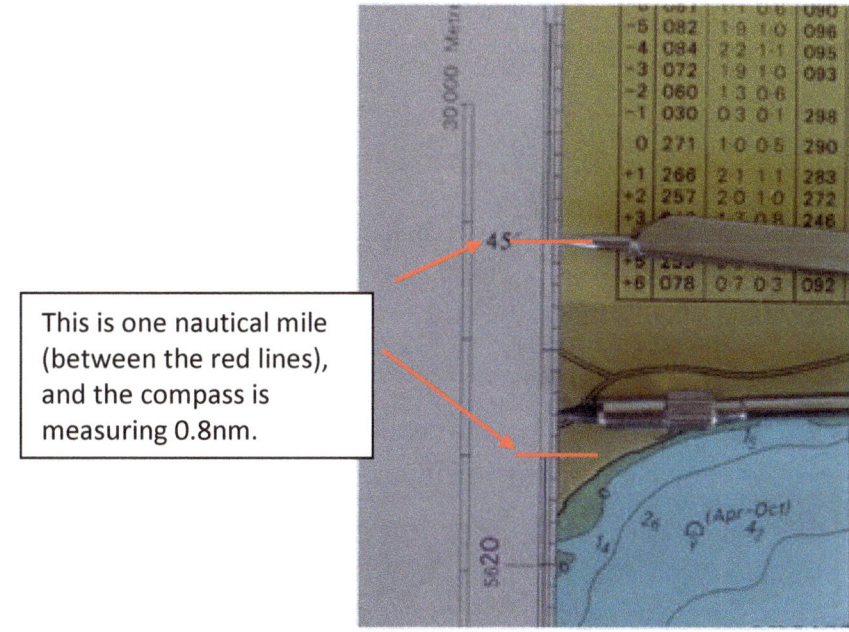

This is one nautical mile (between the red lines), and the compass is measuring 0.8nm.

Plotting

Everyone on board should be able to plot confidently, quickly, and accurately. You may need to see exactly where you are immediately so you can find safe water.

At all times know where your safe water is (i.e. good depth, no obstructions), for emergency collision avoidance or giving room to the stand on vessel. This is very important in busy waterways.

If the boat is going too fast for you to safely navigate, slow down. You can drift for a while if you need to (and it is possible), while you check charts etc. Turn the engine on – turn around, hold station if you have to. GPS has a track method, just double back and stay on that until you figure out where you are and what to do. (Only use the track if you navigated safely along it previously).

Constantly, but not obsessively, assess where you are.

Harbour Considerations

Day or night approach (never enter at night unless a known and well-lit port)

- Does the port have a good buoyage system?
- What's the best approach?

Harbour Timing

Check when you can and can't arrive into your proposed destination. Tides, narrow entrances, passing headlands etc. And the best time to depart. Many cruisers like to leave in the morning to utilise the entire day to settle into the sail but departure in the afternoon can work just as well. Time your arrival, where possible, for daylight hours. Is there somewhere you can 'wait' if it is dark and the entrance is new to you or not a main harbour, i.e. where entering at night is hazardous. (Assume all harbours are dangerous to enter at night, unless you know the harbour extremely well (i.e., traversed the entrance numerous times during the day/night and it is very well lit/marked.))

- Know where you can/can't sail
- Any Traffic Separation Schemes
- Anchor areas
- Prohibited areas

Harbour Back-ups

Highlight and research back up ports along the way. Consider conditions of entry. Have ready a few different options, know the ports' contact details, entrance hazards etc., harbourmaster details/radio channels.

Electronic Navigation Aids

They are just that – aids to navigation. Use paper charts as well. Our electronic charts have put our location on top of harbour walls when we have been in safe water. Check landmarks and buoys with your chart and your position relative to them.

Log Book

Keep the boat's log book in ink. If there is an incident and it is required at a later date (in court) it becomes a legal document.

If you make any errors or changes, cross them out with a single line, ensure the original is still legible, and initial the correction.

During a navigation watch, the main points to be entered are the position of major course changes, weather, unusual occurrences, drills, emergencies, other vessels, communication (radio), etc.

Filling out the ship's log book should be routine.

Example log book entries:
- Date
- Time
- Position (latitude and longitude)
- Wind (strength and direction)
- Speed
- Course
- Barometer reading
- Bilge check
- Engine hours
- Comments (include weather and sea conditions, sighting of other vessels, radio communications and miles to go).

Why they are listed in your log book

- Bilge: The bilge column is just a tick to show it is dry (or approximation of how much water is in there and why). This will encourage you to inspect the bilge regularly and therefore find any problems in the early stages.

- Engine information: In the back of your log book keep a detailed account of all oil changes, filter changes, and engine maintenance and repairs.

- Referencing: Underline or highlight (with a highlighter pen), the destination and departure ports throughout the book to make referring back easier. Highlight fuel calculations, for quick reference.

- Good seamanship: Complete an entry prior to handing over your watch. If the person taking over has not completely absorbed your verbal handover, they can read the last log entry.

- The ship's log book or another folder should contain the operation procedures, location of seacocks, weather, navigation plan, emergency procedures, etc.

- Backup: Log entries should be completed regularly, every few hours at the very least (ideally hourly). This enables you to utilise up-to-date information, which is important if it becomes necessary to calculate DR (Deduced Reckoning). It also helps create a routine that includes a good lookout onboard.

Crew
Each crew member will have good points/bad points, things they do/do not enjoy. Remember that food is important for morale.

Discuss watch schedule and rules so everyone's usual sleep pattern is taken into consideration where possible. Discuss how watches may change.

The crew must know where everything is: e.g. seacocks, gas on/off, harnesses, safety equipment, radio (use), emergency drills (allocate tasks), location of fire extinguishers and how to use them, etc.

Before you set off, explain your navigation plan to the crew. It will help keep everyone alert and interested. Brief your crew. Do the crew know the draft of the vessel? The detail in your brief will depend on their level of experience but every boat is different and they need to be acquainted with your vessel.

Can your crew sail your boat into port if something happens to you? What's the procedure if the engine stops, think, 'what would we do?' (Drop anchor? Use sails? Call for help? Who to?).

What if someone falls overboard (MOB button on the GPS), one person must keep eyes on the person overboard and pointing to them (if you have enough crew on board). How to turn around? Procedure for use of engine with someone in the water.

Account for equipment failure (especially electronic devices) know your, and your crews' capabilities and limitations.

Victualling
Food is a great moral booster on board, ensure you know what your crew like/dislike. Have treats readily available. Easy-to-prepare meals are imperative in difficult conditions, something to just add water to or simply heat up, or open-and-eat food/pre-prepared (If there is bad weather approaching, if there is time, one of the tasks would be to prepare food for later).

Seasickness
Discuss seasickness with crew prior to leaving. Have various methods on board to help prevent seasickness. Electrolytes are important for combatting dehydration.

Sea Berth & Lee Cloths
When underway, the usual bunks and cabins may not always be the most comfortable place to rest. Some sea-states can make the boat corkscrew or just move in a very bouncy or jarring manner. A good sea berth will be situated low down and in the middle of the vessel, although this isn't always possible. In severe weather, do not discount the floor – whatever it takes to get some rest. Fatigue is the main cause for accidents/incidents at sea.

Utilise additional cushions in rough weather. Wedge yourself into the bunk to help aid sleep.

Lee cloths can be made tighter by adding ties to the ceiling from the centre of the cloth at the top of the hem. This creates better stability for the person in the bunk on either tack.

Standing Watches
Schedules: Different schedules suit different people. We started with four hours on, four hours off. As we become accustomed to that, we extend the time to between five and six hours. This way we could both have a good sleep. Friends do three hours on/off. Sometimes after leaving port, one of us may crash out for a short nap, then relieve the other.

A rigid schedule on board, watch-keeping or otherwise, is impossible. Flexibility and adaptability from everyone is key.

When at sea, our routine settles in after three days; sleep requirements vary from one person to the other. Arrange a good routine/schedule that suits everyone on board. Everyone on board must feel they receive adequate and equal rest.

Keep busy, as well as plotting regularly (hourly) and maintaining a rigid watch by sight and sound, complete the log book in full.

Routine checks include (in addition to navigation, weather, lookout, and log book entries)
- Sail trimming
- All lines for chafing, wear
- All rigging, loose, tight, any damage or wear occurring
- Extra checks in the bilges, equipment
- Items down below stowed, nothing loose
- Engine checks (if in use)
- Battery power

Watch Entertainment and Staying Alert
Read with a small red light to maintain night vision.

Listen to the radio, but if you need to use headphones, just use one earplug in. Watch-keeping involves listening too. Your boat is a living thing and needs to be listened to.

Obstacles: Keeping watch is not just about other boats; Fishing Aggregating Devices can be a problem where they are not charted. (A fish aggregating (or aggregation) device (**FAD**) is a man-made object used to attract ocean going pelagic fish such as marlin, tuna and mahi-mahi (dolphin fish). They usually consist of buoys or floats tethered to the ocean floor with concrete blocks. If it is possible, arrange a daytime passage through these obstacles.

Night-time sailing
Sailing at night without a full moon can be very nice too, if the skies are clear and the stars light the water. At times vessels are far easier to spot from a greater distance at night (providing they are lit correctly).

Safety
If you are unsure of anything, always wake your partner or another crew member. If you are the one being woken, never become angry. When your crew catch a fish, gybe, reef etc., be prepared to be woken up to assist. If you become resentful at interrupted sleep, the crew may become too scared to wake you and a dangerous situation could develop.

There is nothing wrong with double checking, especially at night-time when you are tired.

It is too late to tell your mate 'I didn't want to wake you', while treading water!

Rules of the Watch/Standing Orders
Standing Orders are the Captain's instructions. You will decide your own rules, here are a few suggestions:

Wake up the skipper:
- If in ANY doubt whatsoever about anything
- If weather changes

- If new, unidentified noises are heard
- If you can't keep your eyes open
- Sail changes
- Anyone going on deck
- No sleeping
- Manoeuvre vessel due to traffic
- Another vessel comes within 3 miles

Summary of Responsible Navigational Practices
- Use a variety of navigational aids to verify your vessel's position
- Verify GPS systems by radar or 3-bearing fix, or fix by distance/bearing
- Utilise parallel indexing
- Determine estimated position, take into account set and drift and leeway
- Cross check positions by using clearing/danger bearings, soundings, transit bearings
- Assess and take into account the Zone of Confidence
- Fix your position at regular intervals
- Monitor your radio (VHF Ch 16)
- Monitor fatigue and health of crew
- Fully brief new crew
- Update charts and publications
- Compare paper charts with electronic charts
- Prepare and adapt for changes (emergency/weather)
- Plot plan on charts and double check
- Navigation buoys markers with discrepancies double check and report
- Maintain a constant lookout by all available means and situational awareness
- Maintain a log book
- Discuss and agree the plan, changes, etc

Parallel Indexing Using Radar

Parallel indexing is where you set up lines around your vessel on radar that 'float' along with the vessel, thereby you have a visual indication of whether you are on course or not as you monitor your track. These lines are fixed lines relative to the vessel.

An Electronic Bearing Line (EBL) or a Variable Range Marker (VRM) is set parallel to the vessel's course. This line is moved to an object that is conspicuous on the radar (headland in the diagram below), the range indicates the safe limit to pass (0.5nm in this example). You must study your radar manual for full set-up and instructions. This is a simple process which is extremely useful.

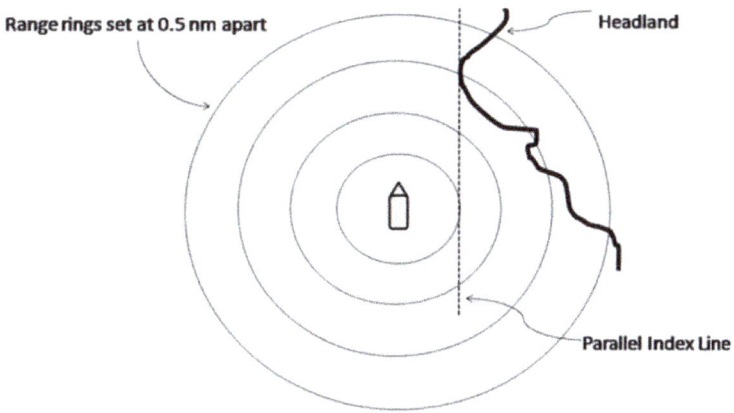

The vessel is in the centre of the range rings, the Parallel Index line is set at 0.5 nm away from the vessel.

Providing you keep the Index line on the headland, you will maintain the most direct course, staying the set distance (in this case 0.5 nm) from the headland.

Bearings

Utilise land edges as they come into transit, or from a set of leads into a harbour (if suitable).

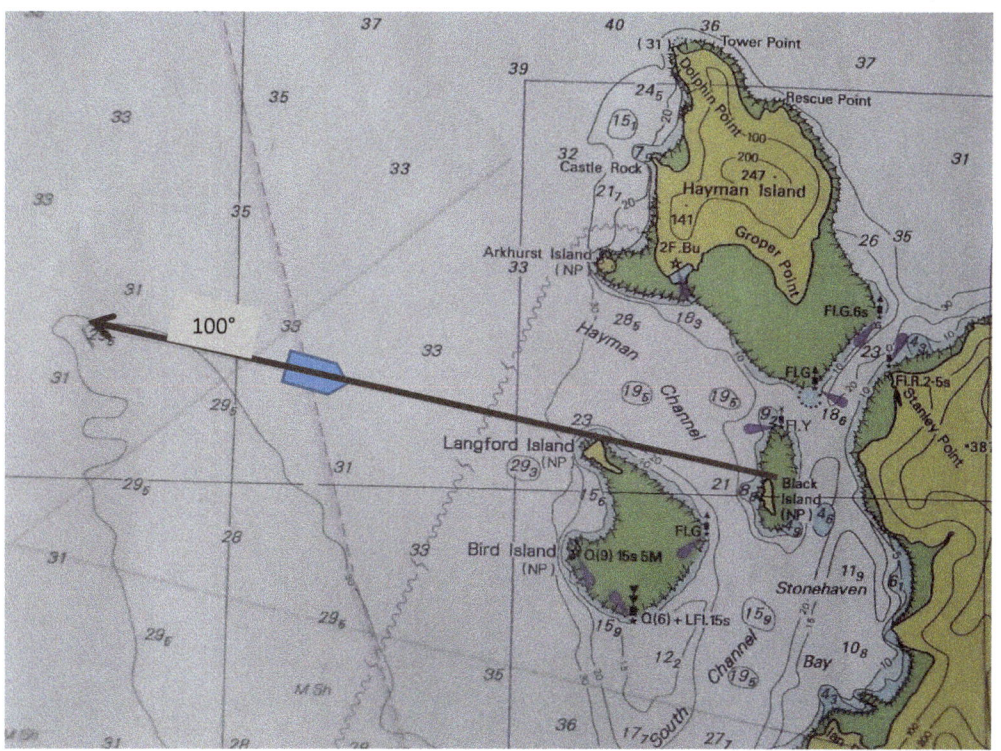

When two charted objects come into line they are in transit. A transit bearing can also be used to obtain a fix in conjunction with another position line. The picture below illustrates a fix with a range (with the transit line). A transit in conjunction with a sounding is not as accurate as a bearing and a range or two transit lines.

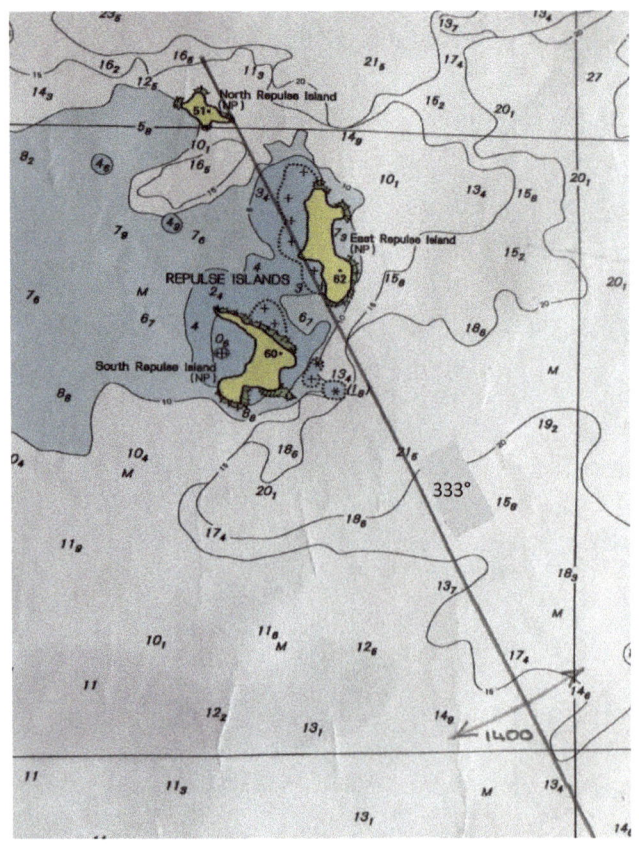

The island tips are in transit. With a radar range (denoted by curved/arrowed line at 1400), this is a good fix.

With the transit bearing you could estimate your position along that line using the depth contours.

However, this can be unreliable, our transit line in this example crosses the 15m contour line more than once!

Clearance Bearings

Clearing bearings keep you clear of any nearby hazards.

Identify a conspicuous mark or headland on the chart, one that you can see and identify at a reasonable range.

On your chart draw a line from the marker or headland you've selected along the safe side of any dangers.

Providing the bearing of the tip of island remains less than 232°T then the vessel will keep clear of the reefs to the south.

This is a True bearing (as are all bearings on a chart). You can convert this clearance/danger bearing line into a magnetic bearing. Then you can monitor this with a hand-bearing compass. The line is there to indicate where you must not cross.

You need to work out what the marker's or headland's bearing would be if you DID cross it. In this case, it would be greater than 232° (varying with how far you crossed the line). Calculate this bearing during your passage planning time prior to departure.

Emergency Preparation
As part of your boat's documentation you should include practices to deal with emergencies. The crew must read this information. Clearly, we cannot prepare for every single eventuality, but general emergencies, such as groundings, do have processes and procedures to follow:

Groundings
If you go aground for whatever reason the first thing to do is secure the ship. If the ship is secure then no matter what happens you have a safe platform and you can stay there (depending on location and weather) for as long as needed.

Sometimes it is possible to remove the vessel from a grounding almost immediately, depending on the tide, sea, and type of vessel. For example, if you ground at the very bottom of the tide, you have full ballast and are in a calm situation (and were going slowly at the time of grounding) the ship should reverse easily. Or if there is a quick way to deploy the anchor in the right position you can kedge off.

On a sailboat, you could swing a weighted/loaded boom out, hoist sail in a beam wind, or ask another vessel to take your main halyard and pull the mast over. Either option will heel the boat and may be free it.

If you do get your ship off quickly, carefully check the hull internally for leaks before doing anything else. Be ready to put her back up if there is substantial damage.

If you are stuck stabilize the vessel and assess your situation as best you can. If you are on a falling tide, transfer weight into the bottom of the vessel and try to deploy the ground tackle (anchor).

If you are in a seaway and you are not ready to act, an option is to deploy the anchors out as best you can. You must try to stop the ship going further onto the reef wherever you are aground.

CHECKLISTS
Pre-Departure Checklists (Extended Cruise)
Week leading up to departure:
- Fill fuel tanks and jerry cans (over time diesel will absorb water, so rotate diesel from jerry cans into main tank and then refill jerry cans with new diesel).
- Check propane tanks/gas supply and purchase more if required.
- Purchase distilled water for batteries.
- Check sea-cocks are functioning and have clear access.

Engine Inspection:
- Coolant
- Oil level
- Belts, tension/wear

- Fuel and oil filters
- Hydraulic oil
- Transmission fluid
- Impeller, hoses, hose clamps

Navigation
- Monitor weather over the week before leaving.
- Obtain long-range weather forecasts, study weather systems.
- Monitor the barometer reading.
- Inform friends and family of your plans.
- Log on with Coast Guard/Marine Rescue, if service provided.
- Plot course on paper charts and enter waypoints into GPS, crew to double check numbers.
- Check charts thoroughly for navigation hazards, highlight.
- Check tide tables and discuss/set departure time.

Other:
- Clean hull, especially the prop, using dive hookah. This is a good time to check the boat thoroughly underwater.
- Check bilge pump and pump float (manual and automatic).
- Check all electronics are operating properly: steering, radar, GPS, plotter, depth sounder, radios etc.

Day before departure
- Top up water tanks.
- Check all items on deck are lashed down properly.
- All items below decks stowed properly, doors and floor locked/clipped in place.
- Rig jack lines.
- Take grab bag out of cupboard and store on bunk (or wherever easily accessed in emergency).
- Remove storm sails from sail locker and place under table in saloon (or accessible place).
- Tie up lee cloths.
- Remove sail covers.
- Uncover steering gear and affix paddle to Aries windvane (if fitted).
- Check autopilots.
- Prepare a meal for first night out.
- Test all running lights.
- Last garbage run.
- Final check on weather.
- Oven gimballed.
- Put out life jackets, foul gear and torches, for the ready.
- Check out with officials (Immigration, Customs, Health, Port Captain).
- Safety briefing with crew.
- Secure and lash dinghy on or below deck.

Shake, Rattle & Roll

No matter how well you have stowed your gear, there will be rattles, rolls, taps and clunks that need to be sorted out. These are very irritating for crew trying to sleep. The tiniest clunk, clunk, clunk, can drive a person a bit batty. It may take time to find everything, as the smallest movement can make a big sound. It is important to seek out the item and correct it. It may be a problem or may develop into a problem if left. A peaceful sleep is very important as far as safety and sanity is concerned.

Stability
Before heading off, think about your vessel's stability. Can water drain off the deck quickly? If you take on a huge wave, this will cause Free Surface Effect (FSE) and affect your vessel's stability. (Free Surface Effect is best understood by holding a tray full of water and trying to keep it horizontal. What happens when the water starts sloshing one way and another?) FSE by way of water on the deck also causes the centre of gravity of your vessel to rise. This negatively affects the stability. Ensure your scuppers and freeing ports are always clear.

Is your vessel trimmed properly? Ideally your boat should be slightly trimmed by the stern (i.e. keep the bow buoyant).

Calculate fuel
There are many formulas and rule-of-thumbs quoted. But the only way to know how much your boat uses is by monitoring it. Keeping notes and adjusting for different conditions. Motoring in calm conditions will use far less fuel then punching into big waves.

You can monitor your fuel usage as you go. In passage planning use the distance measurement and approximate how long you may have your engine on. Having plenty of fuel for contingency plans (different anchorage, bad weather, no wind) is imperative.

Navigation Check List

Check List Before Sailing – Deck
<u>One Hour</u>
Check bilge
Check steering gear (engine room, rudder, wind vane and autopilot)
Check alarm functions (GPS, smoke, radar, etc)
Check trim
Check Radar
Check VHF and SSB radios
Check anchor windlass
Check Navigations lights
Manuals/log books etc available/ready

Open required sea and overboard valves – remember the engine sea-cock
Oil and fuel levels checked
Steering gear tested
Propellers clear

<u>Half Hour</u>
All equipment on board
All stores received and stowed
Paperwork all in order (customs, immigration)

<u>Check Prior to untying/lifting the anchor</u>
Engine running
Raw water exiting over side from engine running
Forward and astern propulsion
Steering – helm free and clear and operating rudder

Check List Prior to Arrival
Contact port control/harbor master if necessary/applicable
Windlass ready to use
Dock lines ready
Fenders ready
Plan discussed, which berth/anchor place – which line first – hand signals
Test astern propulsion before needing it

After Arrival
Radar/GPS etc turned off

Routine Checks
Daily Checks
Stern gland is running coolly if under power and it is not dripping excessively or not at all (depending on the type – traditional/dripless)
Check vessel is clean and tidy (everything stowed)
All equipment and ropes stowed properly
Navigation aids working properly
Hatches and doors closed in bad weather
Emergency exists checked for obstructions (can you get out of your hatch?)
Magnetic compass checked and deviation recorded
Fuel levels

Weekly checks
Radio systems
Battery electrolyte
Specific gravity

Monthly checks
All dogs and seals on all watertight hatches (and doors) checked.
Deck equipment, grease windlass/winches
Safety equipment inspected
Hull visually inspected
Sea cocks

Three monthly check
All the daily and monthly checks
Anchor windlass checked (operate)
Emergency steering checked (operate)
Liferaft checked (visually)

Annual Checks
All three-monthly checks
Internal hull check, particularly bilges and sea cocks
Annual safety equipment surveys (liferafts, flares, EPRIBS etc)

Daily Checks When Underway

Visual checks and/or logging details

These are general items – add your own – e.g. water maker, radar, etc

ENGINE

Item	Date	Date	Date	Date	Date	Date	Date	Date	Date
Oil									
Diesel and fuel tanks									
Coolant									
Batteries (Top up/clean/dry)									
Temperature gauges									
Transmission									
Stern Gland									
Leaks, chaffing of flexible lines, wires, etc									
Engine alignment, stern gland									

ON DECK

Item
Rigging
Lines (chafing – wear and tear)
Sails (chafing, tears, cringles etc)
Steering gear (windvane/autopilot)
Rudder post and bearings

BELOW DECKS

Item	Comment	Crew
Water tanks / water levels		
Radios		
Weather		
Stowing of items		
Stores (pantry and fresh items)		
Pumps		
Sea cocks		

Examples of Appraisal Information
- Charts and Publications (e.g., NP5011)
- BOM for weather and currents
- Routing Charts
- Sailing Directions
- Pilot Books (Recreational boaters: Lucas)
- Tide Tables
- Latest Notice to Mariners
- Port Information Booklets
- Electronic navigational equipment manuals
- Radio and local warnings
- Draft of vessel and height above waterline
- Owner's resource (vessel records)
- Personal experience (handling characteristics, turning circle, speed)
- Mariner's Handbook (e.g. Gandy's, NSW Handbook, SisterShip Navigation Manual/Weather Manual)
- Seafarer's Handbook AHP20
- Ocean Passages of the world (current information)
- Crew certification/details
- Safety Management System
- Routing information
- ACMA Publications (details on restricted areas)
- AMSA Watching-keeping standards
- Owners Resource (agency records, port authority handbooks/regulations)

PLANNING
Radar:
- Use Parallel Indexing (PI) with North Up, Relative motion, Ship centered
- Note: Beam-width distortion to apply: 1° add/subtract as appropriate (total error 2°)

Charts
WGS1984 position can be plotted directly onto this chart.
Depths in metres and reduced to chart datum.
Use DGPS GPS set to WGS1984
Note Pilotage Areas

Speeds
Use GPS to maintain Speed Over Ground (SOG)

Depth Sounder
To remain on during entire voyage, additional checks of position

THE THEORY OF TIDES

What Causes Tides?

The sun and moon have attractive forces, which cause tides. The moon is closer to the sun and therefore much more effective on the earth than the sun.

The moon orbits the earth approximately once every 28 days and largely controls the time of high and low waters. The relative position of the sun and moon determines whether the sun's force increases or decreases the moon's effect on the tide.

When the sun and moon are either in opposition or conjunction this is when spring tides result. This is when the sun and moon are working together to distort the envelope of water surround the earth. When the effects are not in line the sun and moon are in quadrature and neap tides are the result.

Opposition produces a full moon. Conjunction produces a new moon.

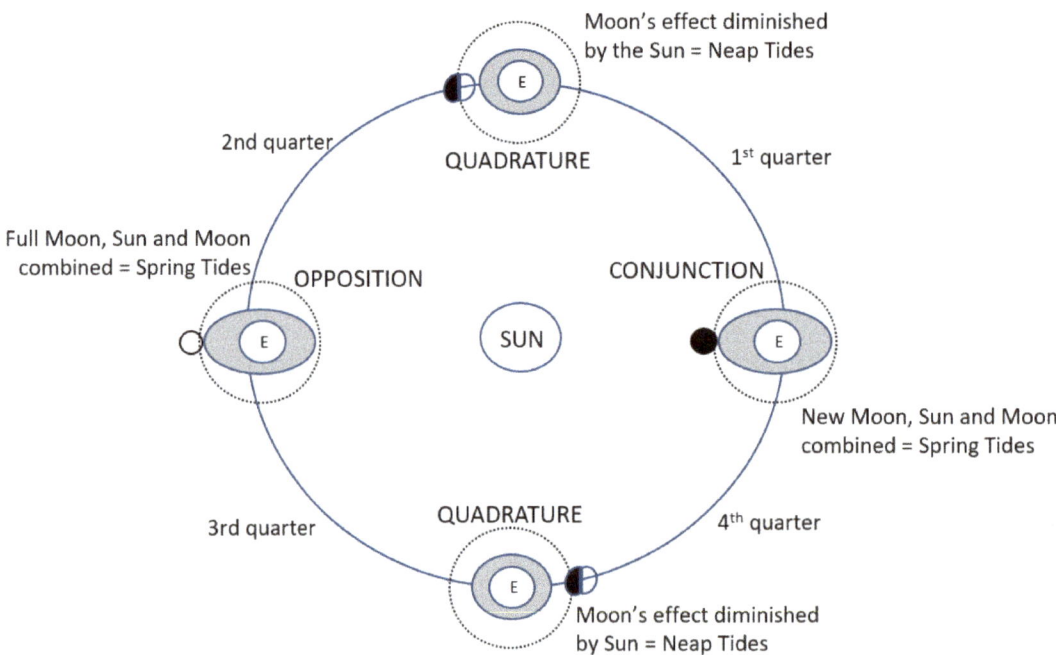

The Effect of Celestial Bodies on Tides

In this diagram, the shape of the envelope of water has been exaggerated. The actual rise and fall of tides in the middle of the oceans is not noticeable on board. However, on the coastline the effects are significant. The shape of the coastline also effects the tidal heights and patterns.

Low atmospheric pressure can increase the height of the tide and onshore winds 'hold-up' the tide. If an abnormal low atmospheric pressure system and onshore winds meet (ie a tropical cyclone) the effects can be devastating.

In maritime we have Chart Datum. Tides are complex, so tidal predications are created to provide a standard set of conditions. Chart datum is Lowest Astronomical Tide (LAT).

There are many other scientific constituents that affect the height and timing of tides. These are called Harmonic Constants. They include facts such as: the ocean has different depths at different locations, the Earth tilts 23° off the vertical, the Earth spins, continents have differing and odd shapes.

Chart Datum

A chart datum is the level of water that charted depths displayed on a nautical chart are measured from. A chart datum is generally a tidal datum; that is, a datum derived from some phase of the tide. Common chart datums are lowest astronomical tide (LAT) (Australia) and mean lower low water (USA). Chart Datum is defined by a level which the tide will seldom fall, meaning the lowest tidal level that can be predicted under average meteorological conditions. Soundings on charts are given below Chart Datum. Drying heights are given above Chart Datum.

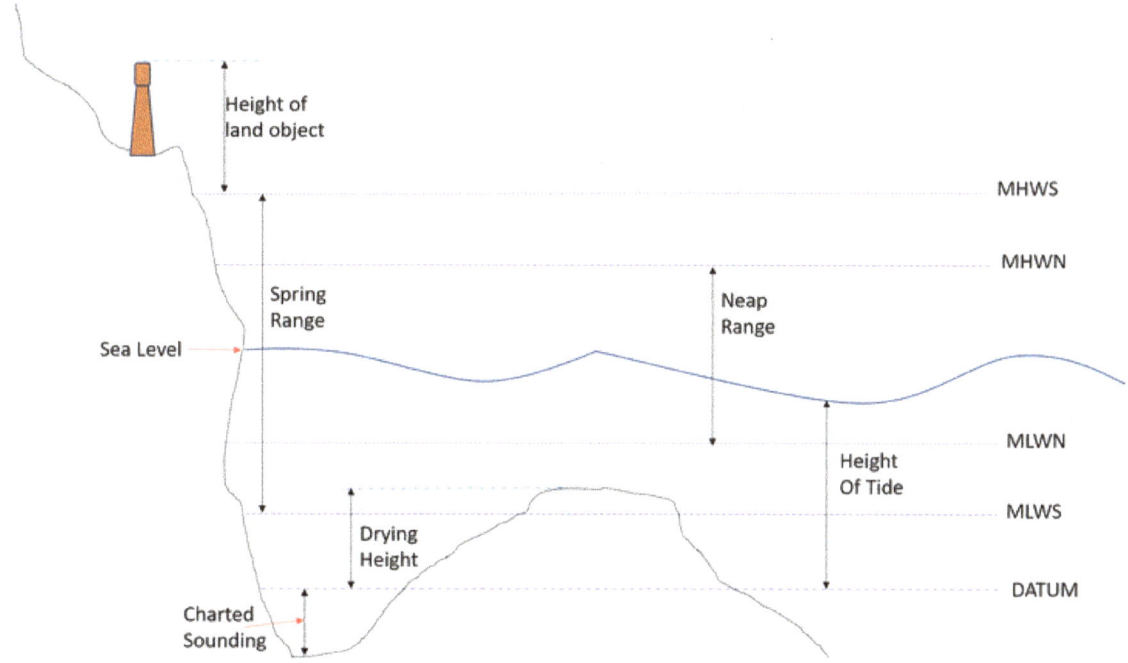

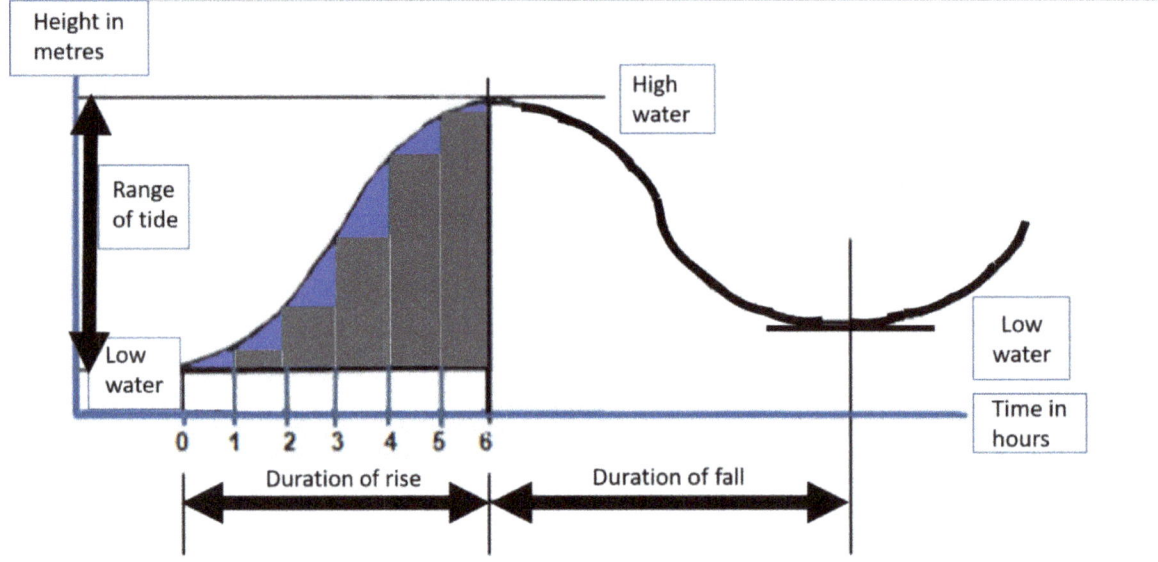

Tide Duration and Range

The Duration of Tide is the time interval between successive High Waters. Range of Tide is the difference in height between Low Water and High Water.

The Duration of the rise is the time interval from Low Water to High Water. The Duration of the fall is the time interval from High Water to Low Water.

Standard Ports

Standard Ports are a reference station where predictions are based on continuous observations, including the changes in conditions due to meteorological conditions.

The information given in the Australian National Tide tables for each standard port is the predicted times and heights of high and low water.

Tide Tables

Standard Port
Example:
To find the time and height of high and low water at Hobart on 16th June 1996.

	JUNE				
	Time	m		Time	m
1 SA	0150	0.8	16 SU ●	0308	0.8
	0806	1.4		0950	1.4
	1204	1.2		1209	1.4
	1907	1.9		1947	1.8
2 ○ SU	0245	0.7	17 MO	0348	0.8
	0915	1.4		1045	1.4
	1259	1.2		1247	1.4
	1958	1.9		2022	1.8
3 MO	0342	0.6	18 TU	0427	0.9
	1020	1.5		1132	1.4
	1412	1.3		1337	1.4
	2053	1.9		2058	1.7

	TIME		HEIGHT	
	HW	LW	HW	LW
		0308		0.8
HOBART	0950		1.4	
16.6.96		1209		1.4
	1947		1.8	

Note: There is no fall in tide in this example due to various reasons: some areas have only one tidal change daily due to variations in pull of celestial bodies, the different effects of gravitational forces, shape of coast line, etc.

Heights and Times of Intermediate Tides
You may need information on the Height of Tide at times other than High Water or Low Water.

For example:
- Depth of water available at your calculated time of arrival at port, there may be a shallow to navigate.
- Calculate the earliest time for sufficient under-keel clearance on a rising tide or falling tide.

To calculate intermediate tides, an easy method is to use Form AH130. AH130 is an L-shaped graph. It is straightforward to use but you must take care with the plotting.

- The uppermost part of the time scale graph is High Water
- You extract the High Water time when looking at a falling tide (plotted at the top of the time scale graph).
- You extract the Low Water time when looking at a rising tide (plotted at the bottom of the time scale graph).
- Scales: If the height of High Water is 5 metres or less, you must use the larger of the height scales. If the height of High Water is larger than 5 metres you must use the smaller of the height scales.
- NEVER mix up the two scales
- Be cautious when plotting decimal fractions.

Intermediate Heights Example:

Using the Tide Table Extract for Gladstone and Form AH130, find the Height of Tide for Gladstone at 0700 hours on the 20th May.

From the daily predictions, the Times and Heights of Tide on either side of 0700 for the morning of that date are:

0231   3.7m (HW)
0914   1.2m (LW)

The following form (AH130) provides instructions.

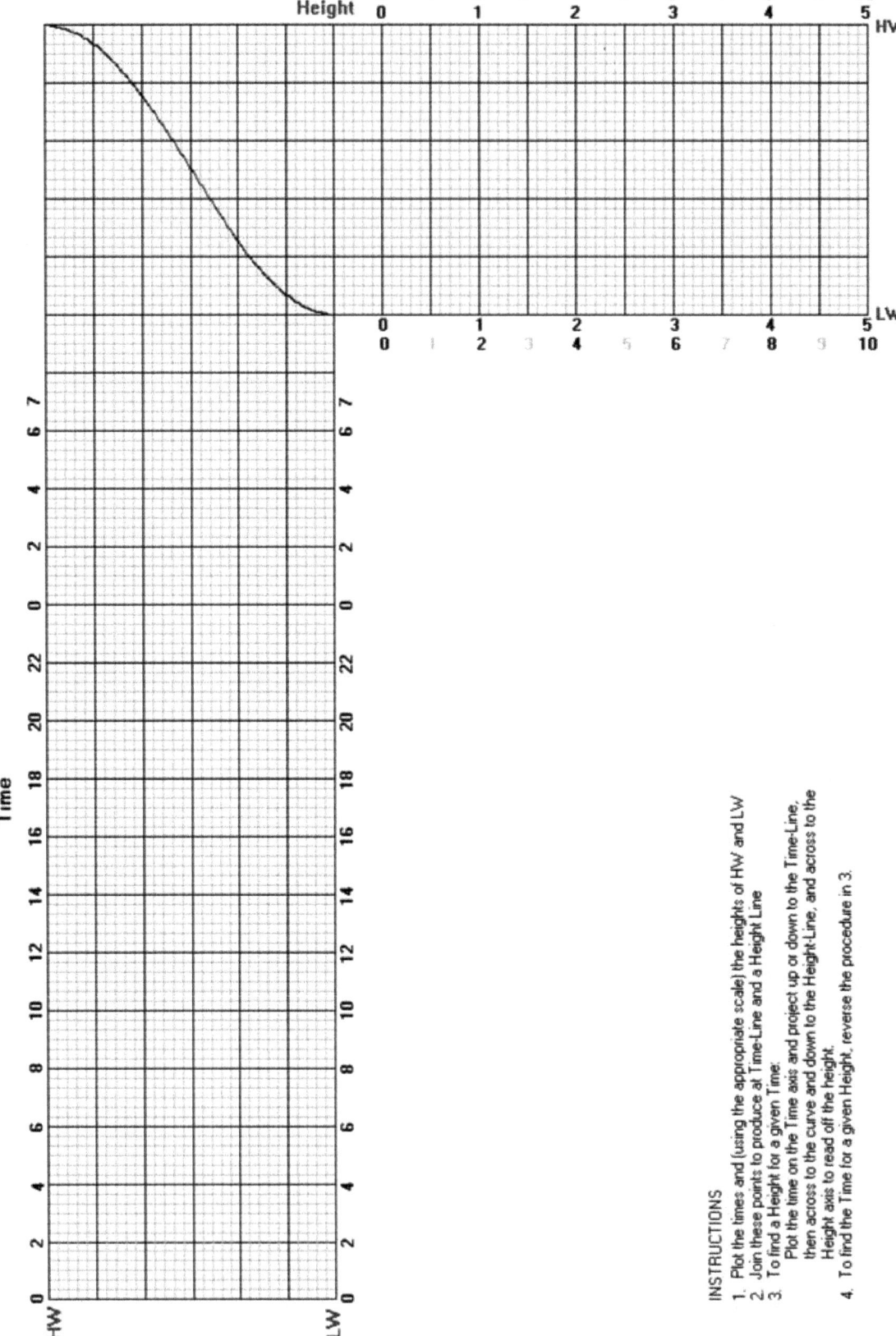

INSTRUCTIONS
1. Plot the times and (using the appropriate scale) the heights of HW and LW
2. Join these points to produce at Time-Line and a Height Line
3. To find a Height for a given Time:
   Plot the time on the Time axis and project up or down to the Time-Line, then across to the curve and down to the Height-Line, and across to the Height axis to read off the height.
4. To find the Time for a given Height, reverse the procedure in 3.

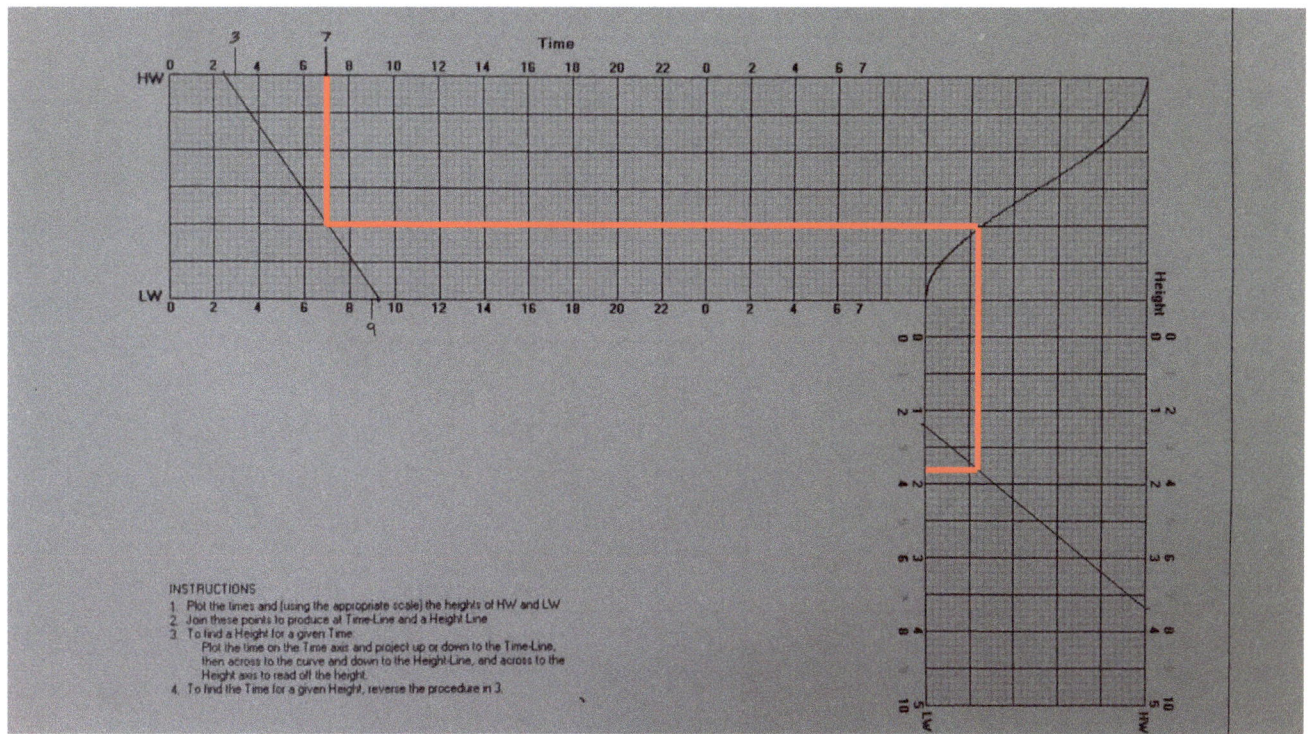

Determining Under Keel Clearance

Firstly, ensure you know your draft.

Secondly, you consult the chart to find the soundings/drying heights.

Remember these are below and above chart datum respectively.

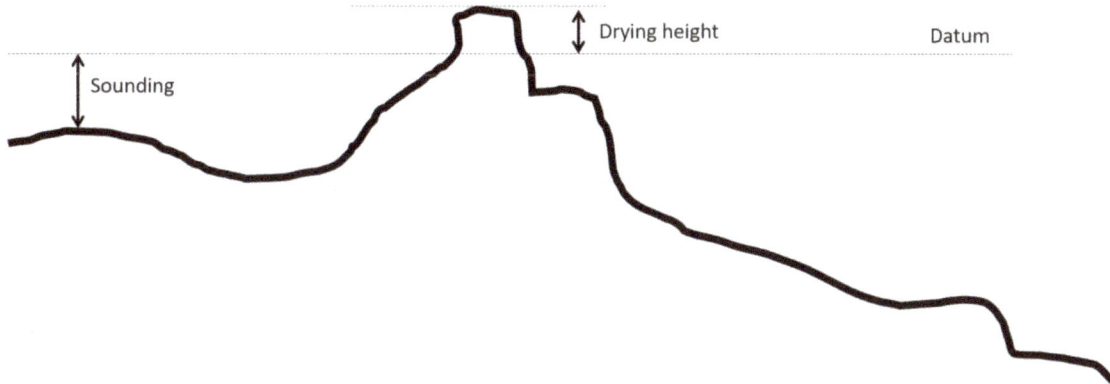

Thirdly, find the heights of high and low water for the area.

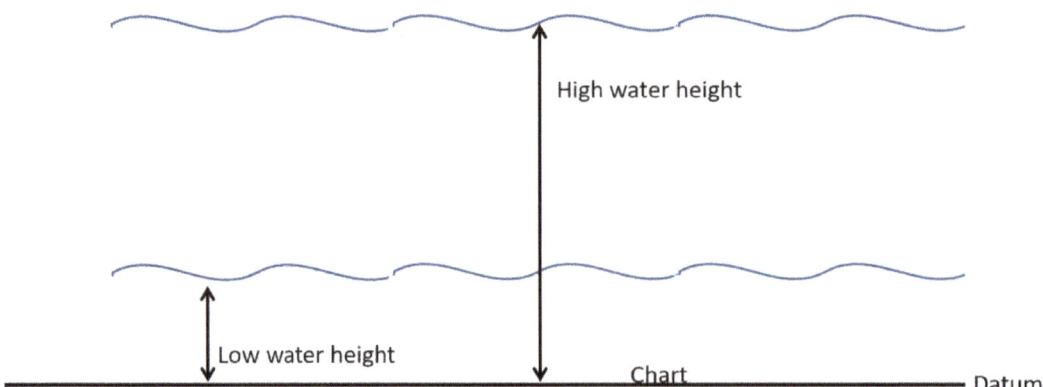

The formula

Under keel = (Height of tide + Sounding) - (Vessel's Draught)

Remember that a drying height is a negative (-) sounding.

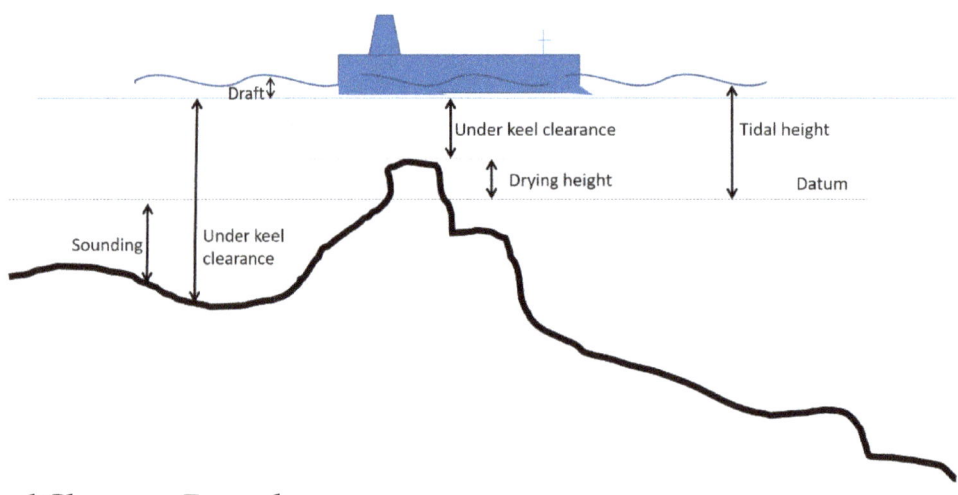

Under Keel Clearance Example

Bundaberg October 16th 2006 on the morning high water (1040 hours) of 2.8 metres.

The vessel's draught is 1.6 metres.

What is the under keel clearance over a rock of drying height 0.9 metre.

Tip: It is a good idea to draw out the picture to visualise the different depths – it doesn't have to be a work of art, just a sketch is sufficient.

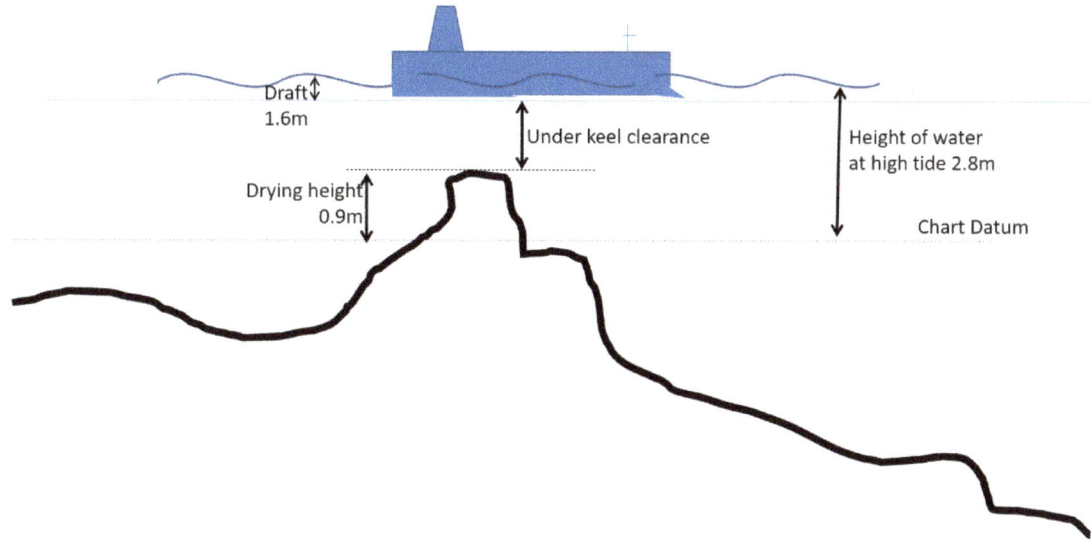

Under keel clearance = (Height of tide + Sounding) - (Draught)

Drying High Tide = 0.9 metres

Drying is a negative sounding, therefore: 2.8 - 0.9 = 1.9

Less your draft of 1.6 metres: 1.9 – 1.6 = 0.3

The under keel clearance at high water (1040hrs) = 0.3 metres

Section Summary

You have worked out tide calculations relating to chart datum. You can now extract times and heights from tide tables for standard ports and apply this information with draft and charted depths to provide a safe keel clearance.

INTRODUCTION TO ELECTRONIC CHARTS

Whether we are on a recreational vessel or a commercial one we all have a responsibility for our boat, crew, and fellow boaters.

No single tool replaces the necessity of sound judgement and good seamanship.

"Charts are expensive!" And so is a boat, a mast, an engine, but would you choose not to have one due to the expense? The right equipment and correct understanding of its benefits and limitations is imperative. If you are involved in a marine incident where additional charts would have helped, they become a cost-effective piece of equipment.

Every piece of equipment at the navigator's hands contains errors due to constant natural and manmade changes, and limitations of our technology and, of course, human error. That's every type of chart – whether official, unofficial, electronic or paper, and every electronic gizmo including GPS!

> *"More than eighty percent of our ocean is unmapped, unobserved, and unexplored."*
> NOAA (National Oceanic and Atmospheric Administration)

> *"With over a billion features in our cartography database, even an accuracy rate of 99.999% would still leave room for some 10,000 potential inaccuracies. No chart, regardless of the source, can avoid this simple mathematical rule."*
> Navionics

All charts are an aid to navigation. We must use eyes and ears and our skill in finding out where we are by what we can physically see, for example landmarks.

We must never go to close to reefs, we must look for breaking waves, and different shading of the water with someone on the bow, and/or up high on rat-lines, with the sun behind them.

An Introduction to ENCs Capabilities and Limitations

Survey

The best of modern surveying methods is utilised for the shipping lanes. Recreational boaters often explore areas where survey information has less confidence (i.e. areas with a reduced 'Zone of Confidence'). Remote areas will have the most inaccurate surveys.

The Zoom Function

<u>Zooming In</u>: Zooming out too far on some Electronic Navigation Charts (ENCs) can mean that some important information is lost. However, do you know that zooming IN too far can be just as dangerous?

Zooming in may reveal a larger scale chart but it can dangerous around isolated dangers.

Every ENC is compiled at an intended maximum scale. At this scale, the maximum level of detail is revealed, while zooming out will progressively reduce the level of detail. None of this affects the accuracy of the chart. Zooming in may reveal a new, larger scale ENC, but this too has limits, and a point will be reached where there is no point zooming in further.

At the intended maximum compilation scale, details which are too small to chart, but which still present a hazard to navigation, are typically replaced by a symbol larger than the charted size of the feature (such as a very small reef). Zooming in to over-scale destroys the relationship between the size of the (now larger) hazard and the size of the symbol.

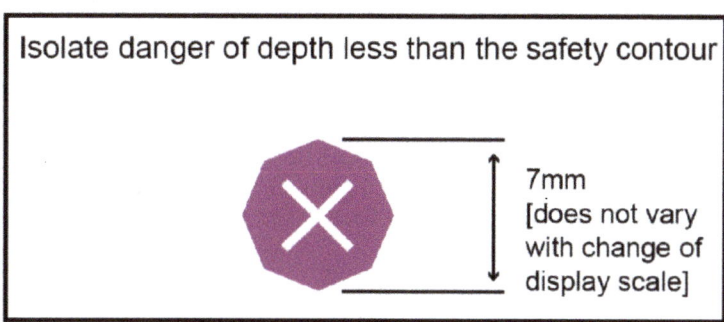

When the ENC is displayed correctly, the danger to a ship close to an isolated danger is clear.

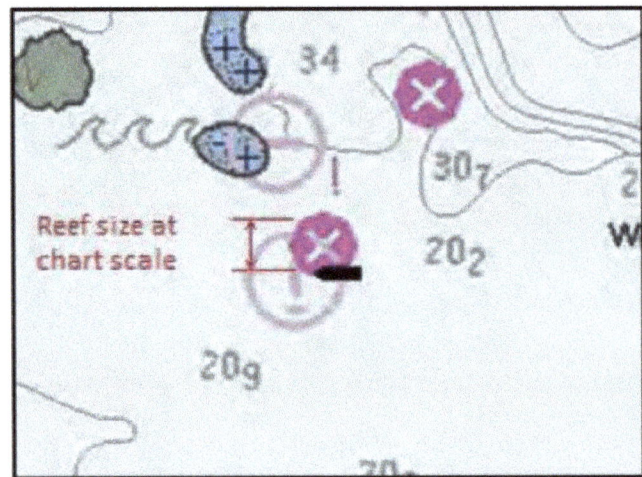

However, when displayed at over-scale, a ship the same unsafe distance from the isolated danger incorrectly appears to be safe because the isolated danger symbol is still the same size.

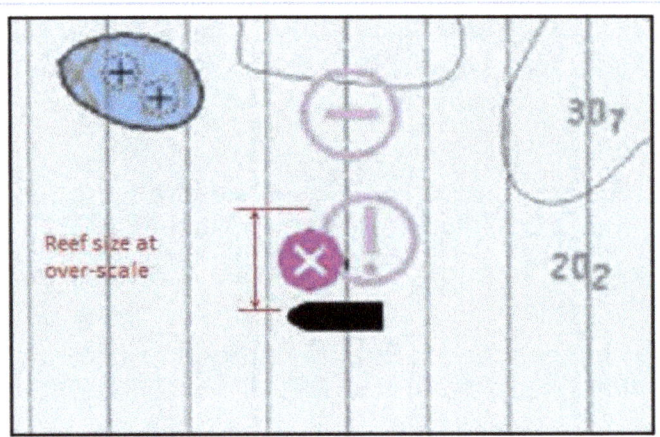

This is not more accurate, and is definitely not safe. The positioning inaccuracy of the isolated danger may be greater than 500 metres.

Routes should be planned to clear these dangers by at least as far as the ZOC category immediately around the danger dictates.

Zooming Out: Zoom out too far and you may switch to a smaller scale chart that does not show all the data.

Settings: You must be confident with all your Electronic Chart Display Information Systems (*ECDIS) or Electronic Charting System (*ECS) settings.

While passage planning you may have to check then un-check settings at various levels of zoom so
1) You can view all the information
2) Your screen isn't so cluttered you miss information
3) Check you haven't zoomed in or out too much

This is why it is advisable to use an overall paper chart for planning at the very minimum.

*The ECDIS is an electronic charting system that is fully compliant with the International Maritime Organisation (IMO) and Safety of Life at Sea (SOLAS). ECS are not fully compliant.

GPS

The GPS is over relied upon and there are certain anomalies that the navigator must be aware of:

GPS - The Position Dilution of Precision (PDOP)/Satellite Geometry

With the advent of Global Navigation Satellite System (GNSS), the Geometry of the satellites is often minimal. The better GNSS receivers today can track more than two satellite constellations, providing them access to many more satellites simultaneously.

BUT not all receivers behave the same. Each GNSS manufacturer has created their own estimated accuracy algorithms. And while accuracy may have improved it can still be 'some' metres out. Add that to a few more metres on a reef on unofficial charts, then very quickly a navigator can find themselves in trouble.

You must check the PDOP every time you take a position. If your GPS receiver does not display PDOP, there will be some indication of poor geometry, check for an icon (read the manual). If there is a high PDOP you are risking positional errors being greater than expected.

The more satellites you use the better the chance that the PDOP will be low. A period of high PDOP is called an outage, usually lasting a short time until other satellites come into view.

Understanding PDOP

PDOP Reading	GPS Displayed Position
2	may give results that are only half as accurate as for a PDOP of 1
3	maybe three times less accurate

PDOP depends on your latitude, longitude, the time of day, the number of healthy satellites and how many of them are available to you.

Remember: the higher the level of Dilution, the bigger the error.

Reliable and Confident

How accurate are nautical charts? The answer is a complex one. The important question is, do you have the necessary skills and equipment to navigate?

All charts contain data which varies in quality. This is due to the age and accuracy of surveys. Surveys in remote areas will be surveyed less frequently than shipping lanes. Charts should show a Reliability Diagram, more often known as the Zone of Confidence, to show the potential inaccuracy of the information.

Disasters

Vestas Wind and the Cargados Carajos Shoal – 2014: The skipper and navigator believed there was no risk of a collision, because they had examined their anticipated route and saw no obstructions. They did anticipate passing a "seamount" with about 120ft of water over it where they expected a change in sea state. Their confidence was based on having viewed the route on one of the vessel's two laptops running charts that did not show that there was a landmass in their path when viewed at medium zoom levels. However, at larger-scale zoom levels the shoal was depicted correctly as a landmass and a hazard to navigation.

Sail Magazine: https://www.sailmagazine.com/racing/vestas-wind-and-the-cargados-carajos-shoal

USS Guardian - Tubbataha Reef 2010

The coastal scale electronic chart supplied to USS Guardian was flawed due to human error on the part of the National Geospatial-Intelligence Agency (NGA). This error mis-located the Tubbataha Reef by 7.8 nautical miles from its actual location. NGA was aware of this error in 2011 and updated a smaller scale electronic chart, but failed to publish a correction for the larger scale chart that the USS Guardian was using when she ran aground.

Southern Fiji, June 2017
The four crew onboard the 60ft Oyster decided to go to Fiji instead of Tonga because of an equipment failure, then activated a distress beacon at 4am after going aground on a reef. "The radar never picked up the reef and the plotter on the radar base said we were three miles off but the two plotters were incorrect by three miles, we just hit the edge of the reef."

Wrong Zooms
From sv Golden Glow on Noonsite

We noticed that the Beveridge Reef appears on our Furuno Chart, but only when it's zoomed in to a map size of 35 nm across the screen (at 40 nm size it's NOT visible).

Navionics and iNavx apps DO show Beverage Reef, but our Earthmate (Garmin) app, the map for our Delorme explorer device, does NOT show the reef.

The Different Charts

Most recreational boaters will be using vector charts (official or unofficial). Navionics, CMap, The Hydrographic Office, etc all use Vector charts.

Raster Charts
- Essentially a scanned paper chart
- All paper chart info is retained
- Easiest to adjust to using (if you are familiar with paper charts)
- They take up a lot of (electronic) storage space
- Everything zooms at the same rate

Vector Charts
- They have been created by 'someone'
- They are only as accurate as the underlying chart they were made from
- Take up a lot less (electronic) space
- Contains additional data

Satellite Programs

Google Earth is not made for navigation. But as an aid to navigation it can be some help.

When using satellite imagery we must remember that it is not up to date. For coral reefs that may not be such a problem, but for sand bars it could be.

Zooming in on a satellite image of coral we can sometimes see shallow and deep areas. But we must remember that some images are affected by cloud cover. Perhaps the sun was at the wrong angle when the image was captured. To help with this problem we can use the history slide bar to find a clearer picture. However, a good internet connection is needed as there is a 2GB cache memory for off line use (Google Earth).

Important

- Maintain a good look-out at all times
- Understand the true accuracy of all your navigation tools
- Plot a detailed route and examine for anomalies
- If you change your route, examine it in full again
- Give reefs plenty of room, even better don't sail around reefs at night
- Use all the tools available (paper charts, electronic charts from different sources, Google Earth (or other satellite charts), Cruising guides, double checking, etc

Appendix

The Pros/The Cons of Electronic Charts

<u>Availability and time saving</u>

Pro: ENCs are sold in packs, so the task of wading through the planning charts to pick off each individual chart you need is no longer necessary (if using e-charts only).
Con: People think that planning charts and checking paper charts is no longer necessary.

<u>Speed</u>
Pro: Quick passage planning – waypoints provided with a touch of screen (i.e. not measuring on a paper chart). Automatic distances, tides etc.
Con: You still need that paper chart. Electronic charts can lack all the detail, be out of date, and be of inferior quality. Which is why they state "Not for Navigation" (except official charts via the Hydrographic Office which are now accepted on commercial vessels provided there is a back-up of paper charts or a second system of official charts on a separate circuit.)

<u>Accuracy</u>
Pros: Updates and corrections are automatic (on most systems).
Cons: On unofficial charts, there can be great delays in updating and not all information is sometimes included.

> The latest confirmed example was a fishing vessel that was damaged on rocks in Bass Strait in Jan 2019 while using unofficial ENCs. The rock was added to the official charts in 2016.

> The worst example was in Brisbane where an entire new area of reclaimed land/rock wall was omitted for five years: Maritime Safety Queensland advised [Hydrographic Office] that a number of vessels had slammed into the rock wall that was missing from their unofficial charts during that time. This came to light during the 2010 inquest into a 2007 death of a passenger in a speedboat that hit the new breakwater at full speed at night. To be fair, the boat driver's ignorance was also a factor.

<u>Continuous Monitoring of Vessel's Position</u>
Pros: Ability to see the vessel's position in real time.
Cons: Over reliance on GPS (as well as e-charts). GPS's errors and inaccuracies must be taken into account.

<u>Stowing</u>
Pros: Far easier to stow than paper charts
Cons: If you don't have two versions of official electronic charts on two independent circuits you will still need paper charts. At the very least small scale, paper charts should be used for overall passage planning and large scale charts for port entries.

The Official Line from AMSA / IMO / HYDROGRAPHIC OFFICE

Scale

Use the largest scale you can, using smaller scale charts is contrary to safe navigational practice. Safety Of Life At Sea (SOLAS) Chapter V regulation 27 – requires nautical charts and nautical publications necessary to for the intended voyage to be adequate and up to date.

The International Maritime Organisation (IMO) states that for a chart (whether electronic of paper) to be considered adequate for navigational purposes, it must be:

- issued officially
- of appropriate scale, suitable for the navigational task at hand
- of the latest edition
- used in its original form, and
- maintained up-to-date, using the latest available notices to mariners or ENC update service.

Official Australian nautical charts

Official Australian paper charts are issued and updated by the Australian Hydrographic Service (AHS) under the 'AUS' series. The series is also largely reproduced by the United Kingdom Hydrographic Office. AHS paper nautical charts are easily identified by their 'AUS' chart number and AHS crest above the chart's title.

A list of authorised AHS chart distribution agents is at www.hydro.gov.au.

Unofficial nautical charts

Unofficial nautical charts should not be used without other charts (e.g. official charts) for voyage planning or navigation.

Unofficial paper charts include (but are not limited) to:

- photocopies
- facsimiles or imitations of official paper charts
- large format commercial printed copies of scanned ENC, and
- paper charts 'assembled' by printing several small portions of a Raster Navigational Chart (RNC)

Unofficial paper charts can be distorted, out-of-date or may omit important navigational features. Scans may not capture all detail shown on the original official chart.

Unofficial copies of official ENC can be at inappropriate scales, contain out-of-date data, miss significant features and information, not have access to a timely or reliable update service, not display correctly or fail to include chart reliability information.

Unofficial electronic charts include those specifically published for recreational use (which typically contain a warning regarding their unsuitability).

Unofficial ENCs

Unofficial electronic charts are required to carry a warning that they are not suitable for navigation without additional charts to check the data. Unofficial charts often do not contain the zones of confidence/CATZOC data quality information layer. Some will even make any poorly charted areas look better than they are;

A fact sheet on unofficial charts can also be found at http://hydro.gov.au/factsheets/factsheets.htm

Responsible navigational practices include:

- Use a variety of navigational aids to verify the ship's position.
- Verify global navigation satellite system (GNSS) positional information by terrestrial means, such as visual bearings and/or by radar.
- Wherever possible, use radar parallel index techniques to monitor a ship's adherence to its planned track.
- Determine the estimated position of the ship, taking into account leeway, set and drift.
- Use soundings, clearing bearings and transits as cross-checks for position fixes and course alteration points.
- Take into account the categories of zones of confidence (CATZOC), which enables an assessment of the limitation of the hydrographic data from which the chart was compiled and the resulting degree of risk.
- Fix the ship's position at frequent and regular intervals, including when a pilot is on board.
- Be aware of and practice human factors principles, including fatigue.

Australian nautical charts and publications
From AMSA: SOLAS Chapter V

Australia's official nautical charts and publications are issued by the Australian Hydrographic Office on authority of the Australian Government.

Be familiar with the operation of your ECDIS

An appropriate nautical chart is one of a suitable scale for the navigational task at hand, noting that the chart's scale determines the level of detail that is provided. Therefore, the largest scale charts produced should always be used. (Note: With observation of 'symbol' distortion).

Small scale charts depict large areas. They are suitable for overall voyage planning and ocean transit purposes. Small scale charts have fewer details about aids to navigation, dangers, coastal features and infrastructure, particularly where larger scale charts exist. Significant depth detail is omitted. Small scale charts are generally unsuitable for navigation in areas less than 30 metres depth, areas adjacent to the coast or close to navigation hazards. Small scale charts contain information about the limits and identity of larger scale charts. Whether in electronic or paper format, small scale charts are neither intended nor suitable for coastal navigation.

Large scale charts should be used when navigating close to the coast, reefs and other navigation hazards. These charts cover smaller areas and provide more detail about depth, dangers, aids to navigation and coastal features. Generally, Australian charts provide continuous coverage at a scale of 1:90,000 (ENC) or 1:150,000 (paper) or larger when navigating within 24 nautical miles of land or major offshore features, except in remote areas.

All larger scale Australian electronic navigational charts (ENC) and paper charts carry Zone of Confidence (ZOC) information, also referred to in ENC as Categories of Zones of Confidence (CATZOC). In ENC this is a selectable layer displayed across the full screen, while the same information is contained in a small diagram on paper charts. This information enables mariners to assess the limitation of the hydrographic data from which the chart was compiled and the resulting degree of risk for navigation. A more detailed explanation can be found in the Mariners Handbook for Australian Waters (AHP 20)—available from www.hydro.gov.au.

The Australian Hydrographic Office publishes the Mariners Handbook for Australian Waters (formerly Seafarers Handbook for Australian Waters) (AHP 20). Information provided in AHP 20 assists ships to operate safely and to comply with requirements of international conventions—for example SOLAS and MARPOL, as well as Australian regulations.

Further Reading

Please note:
You can view the pictures contained within this manual on our website. And the links in the book are also listed on our website. Go to www.sistershiptraining.com then select the Passage Planning Course (either via the Courses Tab at the top of the homepage or via the homepage Course Boxes). On the bottom of the page that details the weather course content you will find a direct link to the pictures/links.

Recommended reading page 32-34 at the minimum:
https://www.yachtingworld.com/news/volvo-ocean-race-team-vestas-wind-grounding-report-published-62609 (click the link where it says 'report available here')

https://www.latitude38.com/lectronic/inaccurate-charts-or-not/

https://www.latitude38.com/lectronic/2017/07/28/#accident-questions-accuracy-of-navionics-charts

https://www.facebook.com/permalink.php?story_fbid=10154541900239488&id=323717144487

A fact sheet on unofficial charts can also be found at http://hydro.gov.au/factsheets/factsheets.htm

Acknowledgements

Special thanks to the Hydrographic Office of Australia for their support and sharing of information. They permitted us to reproduce small sections of their handouts for teaching purposes. Every boater should take the time to read the information in full here:

Everything users hopefully need to know about updating both ENC and paper charts.
http://www.hydro.gov.au/prodserv/publications/AHP24_Edition_4.00.pdf
Everything commercial vessel operators should know about the accuracy of ENC.
http://www.hydro.gov.au/prodserv/publications/ahp20-supplement.htm

Thanks goes to Navionics as well. They provided exemplary 'teacher-training' and answered our stream of questions to help us help boaters wishing to gain full benefits of all their navigation aids.

Disclaimer

While care was taken with the production of this information its purpose is to act as a general guide and to provide information in the form of a broad overview only. SisterShip Training does not accept responsibility for errors or omissions and will not be held liable for any damage or injury arising out of the use or interpretation of any of the material provided in this manual.

www.ingramcontent.com/pod-product-compliance
Lightning Source LLC
Chambersburg PA
CBHW061100170426
43201CB00025B/2425